The Kids-Did-It! Cookie Bookie Cookbook

Fun & Easy Recipes Deliciously Illustrated by Kids!

By Michelle & Glenn Abrams

Featuring Illustrations from the
Kids-Did-It! Designs® Kids' Art Collection

Published by Kids-Did-It! Properties™
www.kidsdidit.com

The
Kids-Did-It!
Cookie Bookie
Cookbook

Fun & Easy Cookie Recipes
Deliciously Illustrated by Kids!

By Michelle and Glenn Abrams

Each young artist represented in the *Kids-Did-It! Designs*® Kids' Art Collection earns a royalty for the reproduction of their artwork.

Art Submission Guidelines and *Art Licensing* Information at:
www.kidsdidit.com

Published by:
Kids-Did-It! Properties™
911 Armada Terrace, San Diego, CA 92106 USA
www.kidsdidit.com

Paperback, *2ⁿᵈ Edition;* ISBN: 978-1461174011

Main Cover Illustration: **A Bird** by Elsa Fleisher, Age 8

Art Direction: Michelle Abrams | *Graphic Design:* Glenn Abrams

iPad Edition Available, ISBN: 978-0-615-39005-5

Also Authored by
Michelle and Glenn Abrams:

Blue Cows & Happy Fruit
Discovering the Artist in Your Child

Lipstick Face
Jessie Abrams, Age 6

This book is dedicated to my
ever enthusiastic spouse and
our two remarkable children,
Jessie and Nick, without
whom this book would
never have been conceived.

Glenn & Michelle

Smiling Robot
Nick Abrams, Age 7

Shape & Chill: Scoop dough into wrap, cover and shape into a long triangle log. Refrigerate for 1 hour.

Cut: Cut chilled dough log into ¼" slices and place on a cookie sheet.

Bake 'til Golden: Bake 12 - 14 minutes

12

350°

...mmmMMmmm... Cookies and MiLK!

Studio Snack Time Liz Masterson & Megan Albe

E ach of the following *Cookie Bookie* recipes was developed to complement illustrations created by Michelle's young art students so, in addition to a collection of deliciously fun, tasty and easy-to-follow baking recipes, this cookbook is also a celebration of the imagination and artistic creativity found in children everywhere!

As a teacher for more than 20 years, Author and Artist, Michelle Abrams, has shared her love for the arts, bringing out the best from her enthusiastic art students.

The resulting images are fresh, cute, often humorous and quite inspirational with many worthy of being called 'fine art' in the tradition of *Matisse, Van Gogh, Picasso* or *Miro*.

Of course, in addition to drawing and watercolor lessons, *Snack Time* with sweet homemade treats was always a studio favorite!

Butterfly
Jeffrey Shutt, Age 6

Author, Michelle Abrams with daughter, Jessie, testing Cookie Bookie cookie recipes.

First Things First

We created the Cookie Bookie to be a fun introduction to baking for kids and assume that an adult familiar with simple baking techniques will cook alongside.

For beginners, most of the recipes include icons that show quantity and size relationships, basic measurements and baking times.

Before you begin, we suggest reading through each recipe first, then gathering all the necessary ingredients.

Baking Basics

We recommend:

Combining all the dry ingredients together before adding them to the wet ingredients.

For best results we also recommend using room temperature eggs, all-purpose flour, and room temperature unsalted butter.

Butter

Preheating the oven halfway through preparation can help conserve energy.

(Butter from Blue Cows)

When rolling cookie dough flat, use a rolling pin on a smooth, dry surface lightly dusted with flour.

To prevent cookies from sticking, lightly coat your baking pan with a non-stick cooking spray or butter. You can also bake on a piece of cooking parchment paper. Any of these methods will work – we have tested them all… many yummy times!

Orange Happy Face   Elyse Bobczynski, Age 3

Recipes

Blue Squirrel Anna Badger, Age 9

Chocolate Chipmunks

18 Cookies

Sift Together:
(in a small bowl)

1 ½ Cups Flour

½ Tsp. Baking Powder

½ Tsp. Baking Soda

½ Tsp. Salt

Beat 'til Fluffy:
(in a LARGE bowl)

½ Cup Butter

½ Cup Granulated Sugar

½ Cup Brown Sugar

Beat In:

1 Egg

1 Tsp. Vanilla Extract

Mix:
Now add flour mixture and mix until blended.

Add:
1 Cup Chocolate Chips

(Optional) ½ Cup Walnuts
Or Macadamia Nuts, or Almonds. No Acorns, please.

Bake 'til **Golden:**
Drop spoonfuls of dough on a cookie sheet.

Bake 14 - 16 minutes

350° Degrees

A Bird Elsa Fleisher, Age 8

Cherry Chirps

18 Cookies

Sift Together:
(in a small bowl)

1 ¾ Cups Flour

½ Tsp. Baking Powder

½ Tsp. Baking Soda

½ Tsp. Salt

Beat 'til Fluffy:
(in a LARGE bowl)

½ Cup Butter

½ Cup Sugar

Beat In:

1 Egg

½ Tsp. Vanilla Extract

Mix:

Now add flour mixture and mix until blended.

Add:

1 Cup Dried Cherries

Form the dough into 1 inch balls, then roll in granulated sugar.

Bake 'til *Golden*:

Place on a cookie sheet. Gently flatten each cookie before topping with ½ Maraschino cherry.

15

350°

Bake 15 - 17 Minutes

350° Degrees

Butterfly Jeffrey Shutt, Age 6

Peanut Butterflies

10 Butterflies.

Sift Together:
(in a small bowl)

1 Cup Flour

½ Tsp. Baking Soda

¼ Tsp. Salt

Beat 'til Fluffy:
(in a LARGE bowl)

¼ Cup Butter   1/2 Stick

¼ Cup Granulated Sugar   1/4 Cup

¼ Cup Brown Sugar   1/4 Cup

1 Egg

½ Tsp. Vanilla

Beat In:
1 Cup Peanut Butter
(either chunky or plain)

Mix:
Now add flour mixture and mix until blended.

Arrange:
Pat hands with flour. Roll 2 big and 2 small dough balls. Press on a cookie sheet, as shown. Add a rolled center body. Dot wings with chocolate chips or sprinkles.

Bake 'til Golden:
Bake 12 - 14 Minutes

350° Degrees

350°

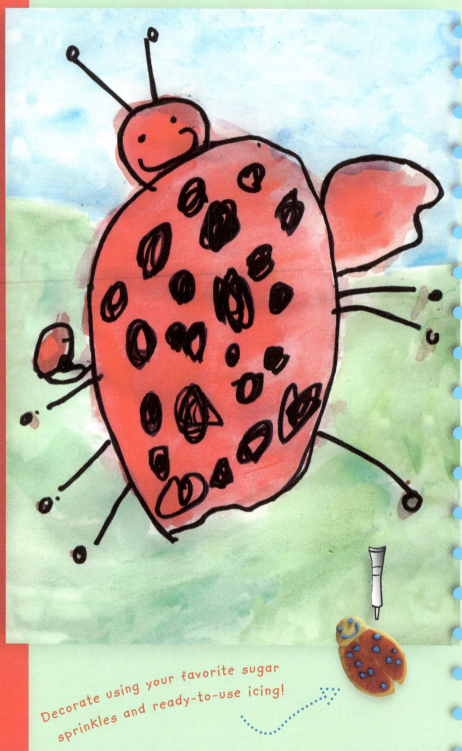

Decorate using your favorite sugar sprinkles and ready-to-use icing!

Lady Bug Dots

18 Cookies

Sift Together:
(in a small bowl)

1 ¾ Cup Flour

½ Tsp. Baking Powder

¼ Tsp. Salt

Beat 'til Fluffy:
(in a LARGE bowl)

½ Cup Butter

¾ Cup Granulated Sugar

Beat In:

1 Egg

1 Tsp. Vanilla Extract

Mix:

Now add flour mixture and mix until blended.

Wrap & Chill:

Scoop sticky dough onto plastic wrap, cover, and form into a ball. Refrigerate at least 1 hour.

Roll & Cut:

Roll out the dough ¼" thick on a lightly floured surface. Cut out oval-shaped bodies, then press a small dough ball on one end to create the head. Cut a ∧ shape at the other end.

Bake:

Place onto a cookie sheet.

Bake 12 - 14 minutes

350° Degrees

Cool, then decorate.

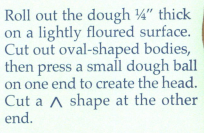

21

Grrr Andrew Asbille, Age 7

DRAGON CRISPS

18 Cookies

Sift Together: *(in a small bowl)*

1 ½ Cups Flour

1 Tablespoon Cocoa

1 Tsp. Baking Soda

1 Tsp. Ginger

½ Tsp. Salt

½ Tsp. Cinnamon

Beat 'til Fluffy: *(in a LARGE bowl)*

½ Cup Butter

½ Cup Brown Sugar

½ Cup Molasses

Mix: Now add flour mixture and mix until blended.

Shape & Sugar: Roll dough into 2" balls, then gently roll dough balls in sugar.

Place on a Cookie Sheet.

Bake 'til Crispy: Bake 14 - 16 Minutes

350° Degrees

Dino Nick Abrams, Age 12

23

1/2 cup powdered sugar mixed with 2 teaspoons of milk makes a nice shiny glaze. Then decorate with sparkly sugar!

Smiling Star Raquel Bobolia, Age 5

Vanilla Stars

12 Cookies

Sift Together: *(in a small bowl)* 1 Cup All-Purpose Flour

¼ Tsp. Salt

Beat 'til Fluffy: *(in a LARGE bowl)* ½ Cup Butter

¼ Cup Powdered Sugar

1 Tsp. Vanilla

Mix: Now add flour mixture and mix until blended.

Wrap & Chill: Scoop sticky dough onto plastic wrap, cover and form into a ball. Refrigerate for 1 hour.

Roll & Cut: Roll out the dough ¼" thick on a lightly floured surface. Cut the dough into star shapes and place on a cookie sheet.

Bake 'til Golden: Bake 12 - 14 Minutes

350° Degrees

Cool, then decorate.

Mix
½ cup
powered
sugar with 2
teaspoons of milk
& drizzle across the
top of cooled cookies.

Flowers Stephen DeVito, Age 7

Triangle Tea Treats

24 Cookies

Sift Together:
(in a small bowl)

2 Cups Flour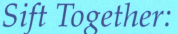

¼ Tsp. Baking Powder

¼ Tsp. Salt

Beat 'til Fluffy:
(in a LARGE bowl)

½ Cup Butter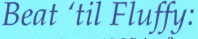

½ Cup Sugar

Beat In:

1 Egg

½ Tsp. Vanilla

(optional) ½ Tsp. Ground Ginger

Mix: Now add flour mixture and mix until blended.

Add: ¼ Cup Chopped Candied or Crystallized Ginger

(optional)

Shape & Chill: Scoop dough into plastic wrap, cover and shape into a long triangle log. Refrigerate for 1 hour.

Cut: Cut chilled dough log into ¼" slices and place on a cookie sheet.

Bake 'til Golden: Bake 12 - 14 minutes 350° Degrees

27

"Give a monkey a Mookie...

and they'll ask for a glass of milk!"

Monkey Stephen DeVito, Age 9

28

MookieChewz

Makes 16 muff... uh... *let's see...*

...it's not a muffin, it's not a cookie, it's a...

Sift Together:
(in a small bowl)

1 ½ Cups Flour

½ Tsp. Baking Powder

½ Tsp. Baking Soda

½ Tsp. Salt

Beat 'til Fluffy:
(in a LARGE bowl)

½ Cup Butter

½ Cup Granulated Sugar

½ Cup Brown Sugar

Beat In:

1 Egg

1 Tsp. Vanilla Extract

Mix:

Now add flour mixture and mix until blended.

Mix:
(In a small bowl)

¼ Cup Granulated Sugar

1 Tsp. Cinnamon

Roll & Bake:

Form spoonfuls of dough into balls, then roll them in the cinnamon and sugar mixture. Place them in a greased muffin pan.

15

Bake 14 - 16 minutes

350°

350° Degrees

Pretty Bird Jessie Abrams, Age 12

Bird Nests

18 Nests

Beat 'til Shiny: *(about 2 minutes in a LARGE bowl)*

2 Large Egg Whites (room temperature)

No yolks!

1 Pinch of Salt

¼ Cup Sugar

Gently Fold In: 3 Cups Dry Shredded Coconut, until just mixed together.

Drop spoonfuls onto parchment paper on a cookie sheet.

Bed Time: With your thumb gently press the center of the cookie to create a bird bed, then sprinkle a few strands of loose coconut on top.

Bake 'til Golden: Bake 20 - 25 minutes. 325° Degrees

20
325°

Lay Eggs: Cool! Then add marshmallow chicks or candy eggs.

If you wish, glaze with 1/2 cup powdered sugar mixed with 2 teaspoons of milk and a drop of red food coloring, then top with colored sugar sprinkles.

Heart Maggie McGregor, Age 7

Sweethearts

18 Cookies

Sift Together: 1 ¾ Cups Flour

(in a small bowl)

½ Tsp. Baking Powder

¼ Tsp. Salt

Beat 'til Fluffy: ½ Cup Butter 1 Stick

(in a LARGE bowl)

¾ Cup Granulated Sugar

Beat In: 1 Egg

1 Tsp. Vanilla Extract

Mix: Now add flour mixture and mix until blended.

Wrap & Chill: Scoop sticky dough into plastic wrap, cover and form a ball. Chill at least 1 hour.

Roll & Cut: Roll out the dough ¼" thick on a lightly floured surface, then cut into heart shapes and place on a cookie sheet.

Bake 'till Gold: Bake 12 - 14 minutes 350° Degrees

Cool, then decorate.

Colorful Heart Bryce Lewis, Age 6

Monster Mish-Mashes

24 Cookies

Sift Together: *(in a small bowl)*
1 Cup Flour
½ Tsp. Salt
½ Tsp. Baking Powder
½ Tsp. Baking Soda

Beat 'til Fluffy: *(in a LARGE bowl)*
½ Cup Butter (one stick)
½ Cup Granulated Sugar
½ Cup Brown Sugar

Beat In:
1 Egg
½ Tsp. Vanilla

Mix: Now add flour mixture and mix until blended.

Add Fun Stuff:
½ Cup Oatmeal (not quick cooking)
1 Cup Chocolate Chips

½ Cup Dried Apricots (Roughly Chopped)
½ Cup Dried Cranberries (or Dried Cherries)
1 Cup Toasted Almonds (Roughly Chopped)

Bake: Spoon onto cookie sheet
Bake 14 - 16 minutes
350° Degrees

15
350°

Circus Train Anna Badger, Age 7

Choo-Choo Chewy Brownies

1 Dozen

(Yea! No Beater Required.)

Melt in Microwave:
(75 SECONDS in a LARGE bowl)

1 Cup Chocolate Chips

¾ Cup Butter

Stir:
Stir until smooth as chocolate melts.

Add:
¾ Cup Sugar

¾ Cup Brown Sugar

Whisk in:
3 Eggs - one at a time.

1 ½ Tsp. Vanilla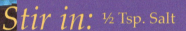

Stir in:
½ Tsp. Salt

¾ Cup Flour

Bake:
Butter an 8" x 8" glass baking dish and line with baking parchment.

Coat the parchment with butter or non-stick cooking spray, then pour the batter into the dish.

Bake about 40 minutes

350° Degrees

(until a toothpick poked in the center comes out with just a few crumbs.)

40

350°

Cool & Cut:
Let cool completely, then lift out & cut.

(waiting is hard ...but worth it.)

Tango Pig Nate Perdue, Age 6   *Big Pig* Gina Barba, Age 5

Peppermint Pig Puffs

12 Little Pigs

Beat 'til Frothy: *(in a LARGE bowl)* 3 Egg Whites *(room temperature)*

No yolks!

Sprinkle: 1 Tsp. Cornstarch

Slowly Beat In: ¾ Cup Granulated Sugar *(a tablespoon at a time)*

3/4 Cup

Beat the egg mixture until it's stiff and shiny.

Crispy outside...
Puffy inside...
...mmmmmm...

Add In: ½ Tsp. Peppermint Flavor
½ Tsp. White Vinegar

Fold In: 4 Drops Red Food Coloring *(using a spatula)*

Dollop onto parchment paper on a cookie sheet.

Gently top with Crushed Peppermint.

Bake 'til Puffed: Preheat the oven. Bake for 1 ½ Hours 200° Degrees

1 ½ Hours
200°

m m.m m mmm: Then **turn off** the oven and leave the puffs inside the oven for one more hour to set.

1 Hour
0°

Baa

Baa

Baa
Sheep
Anna Badger,
Age 9

Baa
Sheep
Kasey Hutcheson, Age 7

Baa

Baa
Sheep
Kelsey Rhoads, Age 10

Fast Sheep
Michele Miller, Age 10

Shy Sheep
Stephen Divito, Age 9

Curious Sheep
Jeff Shutt, Age 8

40

Lamb Jams

12 Cookies

Sift Together:
(in a small bowl)

1 ¾ Cups Flour

½ Tsp. Baking Powder

¼ Tsp. Salt

Beat 'til Fluffy:
(in a LARGE bowl)

½ Cup Butter

¾ Cup Sugar

Baa

Blue Tailed Sheep
Ashley Mondfrans, Age 11

Beat In:

1 Egg

1 Tsp. Vanilla Extract

Mix:

Now add flour mixture and mix until blended.

Wrap & Chill:

Scoop sticky dough onto plastic wrap, cover and form a ball. Chill at least 1 hour.

Baa

Roll & Jam:

Roll out the dough into a rectangle ¼" thick. Coat with a thin layer of your favorite jam and roll into a log.

Cut:

Cut log into ½" thick slices and place on a cookie sheet.

Bake 'til Cute:

Bake 14 - 16 minutes

350° Degrees

350°

Yummmy, our favorite!

Moon Max Hutcheson, Age 9

Moon Michele Miller, Age 11

42

MOON MELTS

12 Cookies

Sift Together:
(in a small bowl)

1 Cup Flour
⅓ Cup Cocoa
¼ Tsp. Baking Powder
¼ Tsp. Salt

Beat 'til Fluffy:
(in a LARGE bowl)

½ Cup Butter
½ Cup Granulated Sugar

Beat In:

1 Egg
½ Tsp. Vanilla Extract

Mix: Now add flour mixture and mix until blended.

Shape & Chill: Scoop the dough into plastic wrap, cover and shape into a 3" diameter log. Refrigerate at least 1 hour.

Cut: Cut log into ¼" thick slices and place onto a cookie sheet.

Bake: Bake 12 - 14 minutes 350° Degrees

Cool 'n Spread: Cool, then dollop Marshmallow Cream between two cookies!

44

Art &
Artist Index

Sheeped Emma Griste, Age 7

In addition to learning
the fundamentals of art
and design, every young
artist represented in the
Kids-Did-It! Designs'
kids' art collection also
earns royalties for the reproduction of their work.

For art submission guide-
lines, art licensing que-
ries and other information,
please go to:

www.kidsdidit.com

Artist	Illustration Title
Abrams, Jessie, Age 6	*Lipstick Face*
Abrams, Nick, Age 7	*Smiling Robot*
Mazur, Conrad, Age 7	*Conrad*
Fleisher, Elsa, Age 6	*Elsa*
Yap, Andrew, Age 6	*Blue Cow*
Bobczynski, Elyse, Age 3	*Orange Happy Face*
Badger, Anna, Age 9	*Blue Squirrel*
Fleisher, Elsa, Age 8	*A Bird*
Shutt, Jeffrey, Age 6	*Butterfly*
Hawk, Emily, Age 4	*Red Lady Bug*
Asbille, Andrew, Age 7	*Grrrr*
Abrams, Nick, Age 12	*Dino*
Bobolia, Raquel, Age 5	*Smiling Star*
DeVito, Stephen, Age 7	*Flowers*
DeVito, Stephen, Age 9	*Monkey*
Abrams, Jessie, Age 12	*Pretty Bird*
McGregor, Maggie, Age 7	*Heart*
Lewis, Bryce, Age 6	*Colorful Heart*
Raser, Keaton, Age 8	*Chimera*
Badger, Anna, Age 7	*Circus Train*
Perdue, Nate, Age 6	*Tango Pig*
Barba, Gina, Age 5	*Big Pig*
Bowen, Sarah, Age 7	*Piggle*
Hutcheson, Kasey, Age 7	*Sheep*
Badger, Anna, Age 9	*Sheep*
Miller, Michele, Age 10	*Fast Sheep*
DeVito, Stephen, Age 9	*Shy Sheep*
Rhoads, Kelsey, Age 10	*Sheep*
Shutt, Jeffrey, Age 6	*Curious Sheep*
Mondfrans, Ashley, Age 11	*Blue Tail Sheep*
Griste, Emma, Age 7	*Sheeped*
Hutcheson, Max, Age 9	*Moon*
Miller, Michele, Age 11	*Moon*
Van Woy, Lauren, Age 9	*Earth*

Art Teacher, Michelle Abrams, with
her assistant Nick and Students

About the Authors

Michelle Abrams
Artist, Art Instructor
Abrams Art Studio

Michelle, a mother of two artists, has a Master of Fine Arts degree from *Yale University* and a broad range of professional experience in the creative arts, including animating for *Sesame Street*, serving as a multimedia Creative Director, and managing her own design studio.

Currently she is a professional painter and art instructor living in Southern California.

www.michelleabrams.com

Glenn Abrams
President
Kids-Did-It! Properties

A graduate of the *Rhode Island School of Design*, throughout his career Glenn has served as Designer, Creative Director and Event Producer on a wide variety of multimedia, marketing communication and entertainment projects.

In 1996 Glenn partnered with his wife, Michelle, to create *Kids-Did-It! Properties*, a California publisher and design studio that also licenses reproduction rights to their growing **Kids-Did-It! Designs**® art collection of fresh and colorful illustrations, most created by Michelle's young art students, ages 3 to 14.

www.kidsdidit.com

CPSIA information can be obtained
at www.ICGtesting.com
Printed in the USA
LVHW070333151121
703355LV00015B/102